DIGESTING THE CHILD WITHIN

Author of

Don't Worry, He Won't Get Far on Foot:
The Autobiography of a Dangerous Man

Do Not Disturb Any Further

DIGESTING THE CHILD WITHIN

AND OTHER CARTOONS TO LIVE BY

JOHN CALLAHAN

Quill
William Morrow
New York

For the K-Man

Copyright © 1991 by John Callahan

All rights reserved. No part of this book may be reproduced or utilized in any form or by any means, electronic or mechanical, including photocopying, recording, or by any information storage or retrieval system, without permission in writing from the Publisher. Inquiries should be addressed to Permissions Department, William Morrow and Company, Inc., 1350 Avenue of the Americas, New York, N.Y. 10019.

It is the policy of William Morrow and Company, Inc., and its imprints and affiliates, recognizing the importance of preserving what has been written, to print the books we publish on acid-free paper, and we exert our best efforts to that end.

Library of Congress Cataloging-in-Publication Data

Callahan, John.
    Digesting the child within / by John Callahan
        p.   cm.
    ISBN 0-688-09488-0
    1. Life—Caricatures and cartoons. 2. American wit and humor,
Pictorial. I. Title.
NC1429.C23A4   1991
741.5′973—dc20   91-16896
                                                                    CIP

Printed in the United States of America

        13 14 15 16 17 18 19 20

For information regarding Callahan T-shirts, mugs, and other products, please contact:

    Levin Represents
    Deborah Levin
    234½ Hampton Drive
    Venice, California 90291

Acknowledgments

I'd like to thank the following people for their unending help and support: Deborah Levin, Larry Wobbrock, Mark Grimes, Jerry Fine, Richard Pine, Laura Mason, and especially to my editor, Liza Dawson, who *still* hasn't pushed me down the stairs.

"I'm O.K., you're O.K."

— Thomas A. Harris

"I'm O.K., you're K.O.'d"

— John Callahan

"Someday, son, all this will be yours!"

11

THE LOW SELF-ESTEEM ENGINE

CALLAHAN

MOSES PARTING THE "BIG GULP"

CALLAHAN

15

SEX ADDICTS ANONYMOUS

CALLAHAN

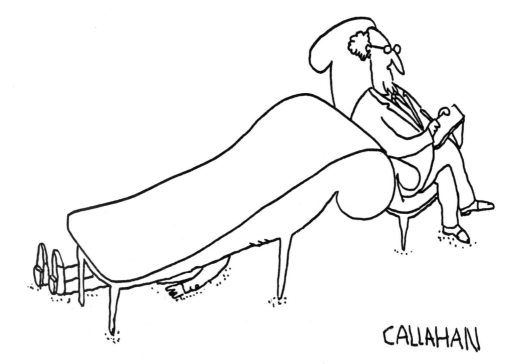

"What drove you over the edge?"

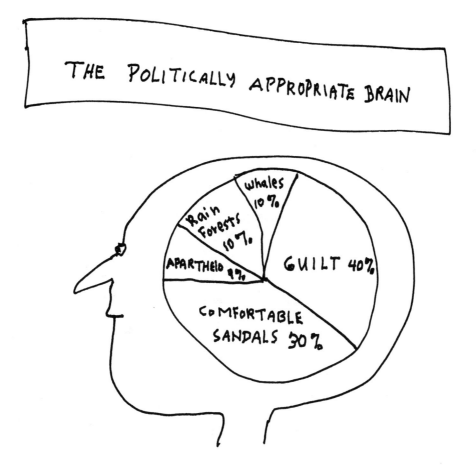

THE POLITICALLY APPROPRIATE BRAIN

whales 10%

Rain Forests 10%

APARTHEID 9%

GUILT 40%

COMFORTABLE SANDALS 30%

CALLAHAN

"I dreamt I had a Harem, but they all wanted to talk about the relationship."

IT IS A LITTLE KNOWN FACT THAT
LEO BUSCAGLIA HUGS PEOPLE
TO DRY HIMSELF OFF.

CALLAHAN

"Now, isn't that better than that old canned liver?"

CALLAHAN

CALLAHAN

"Could be a good career move!"

"Well, darling, it looks like the stars have fallen from
the sky, the rivers have all run dry, and the poets have
run out of rhymes. Guess I don't have to love
you anymore."

"Miss Shackly, please bring me a larger chair."

"Help! I've fallen and I can't get up!!"

"You read about these things happening to other people!"

"As manager of the hotel I promise I will personally
find you a room with an accessible bathroom!!!"

"I'll have what I'm having."

CALLAHAN

"Finish your vegetables! There are children in
Beverly Hills with eating disorders."

CALLAHAN

"Your order is not ready, nor will it ever be."

44

"I now pronounce you man and wife, if you don't
mind putting a label on it."

"I wonder if you'd mind giving me directions. I've never been sober in this part of town before."

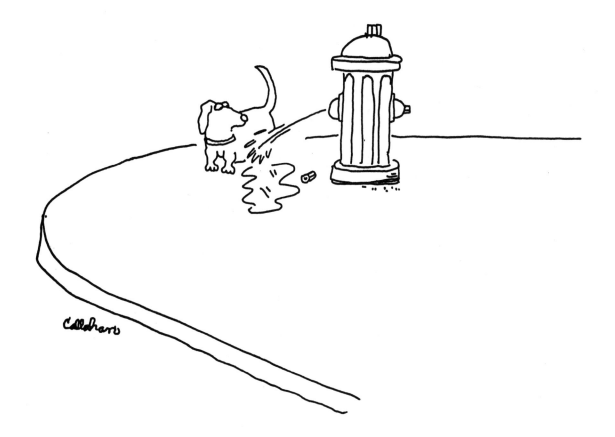

"Daddy! Your barn door is open!"

"Your table is ready."

"It was him or me!"

CALLAHAN

"Now get out there & rake up those fallen limbs!"

CALLAHAN

"Eating the apple couldn't have bothered him that much. It must have been the fact that I fucked you."

"Yes!! For the hundred and fiftieth time! We're burning in hell!!!"

"My name is Mort and I represent Chuck who's an alcoholic."

CALLAHAN

60

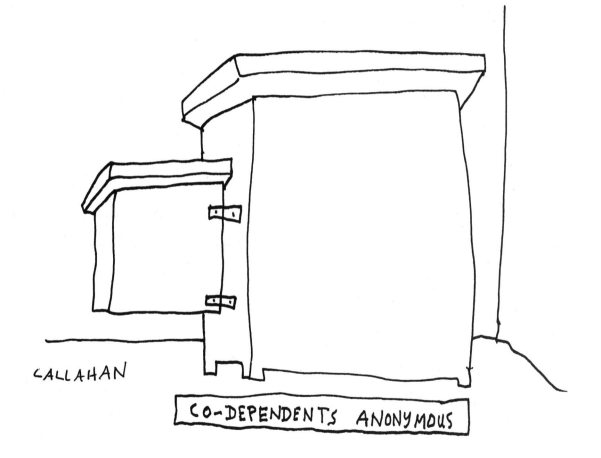

CALLAHAN

CO-DEPENDENTS ANONYMOUS

CALLAHAN

"...and I have difficulty getting close to people..."

RICHARD'S LONELINESS ONLY DEEPENED AFTER SYLVIA'S HELIUM BREAST IMPLANTS.

CALLAHAN

HANNIBAL CROSSING HIS WIFE.

CALLAHAN

"Dammit! I resent being treated as if I were sober!"

S. A. D. (seasonal affected disorder)

CALLAHAN

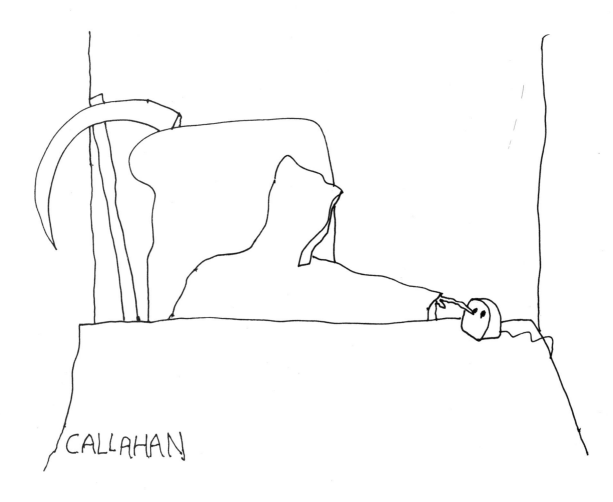

"Miss Jenkins, please die."

"Jenkins, you've been spending far too much time
at the water-cooler!"

CALLAHAN

"It doesn't seem like Christmas without snow!"

CAUTION: MIME FIELD

CALLAHAN

79

80

CALLAHAN

"...and we've arranged a window seat for your dog
so you can enjoy the view!!"

"Let's talk a little about that hollow feeling."

"Your order will be ready when I yell, 'Mother-fucker.'"

I think I was an alcoholic...

Rated PG—13

BY JOHN CALLAHAN

Waiting for a place to happen.
The very first time I drank I got drunk (age 11).

Once I started drinking I couldn't stop. Often I got sick.

I couldn't imagine life without alcohol. Restless and
bored when sober, I managed to quit for brief periods
but I felt tentative about my sobriety.

Booze made me feel normal and uninhibited. It gave
me courage to do things I could never do sober.

A. Ill-advised sexual encounters . . .

B. Bladder problems on the bus...

C. In jail for a minor car wreck at 17, I ended up
in a cell with a child molester who looked like Peter Lorre.

As I got older my drinking followed a fairly pre-
dictable pattern.

**Anyone could see I was in trouble and I resented
having it pointed out.**

After I was paralyzed at 21 in yet another car accident
(my driver and I were both drunk), my drinking
only increased.

**After my accident, I lived in nursing homes for three
years, drinking hard and becoming more and more bitter.**

One night my friend Jay pushed me home from a
bar. Drunk, we did not notice my foot was
dragging beneath my wheelchair.

The nursing home attendants removed my shoes and
discovered my toes had been nearly scraped
off. I was tossed out on my ear.

Moving into an apartment my drinking got worse.
My alcoholic attendant and I drank together.

I discovered I had lost complete control of my drinking.
Time after time I'd take that first drink knowing
it would lead to miserable drunkenness and
horrendous withdrawal.

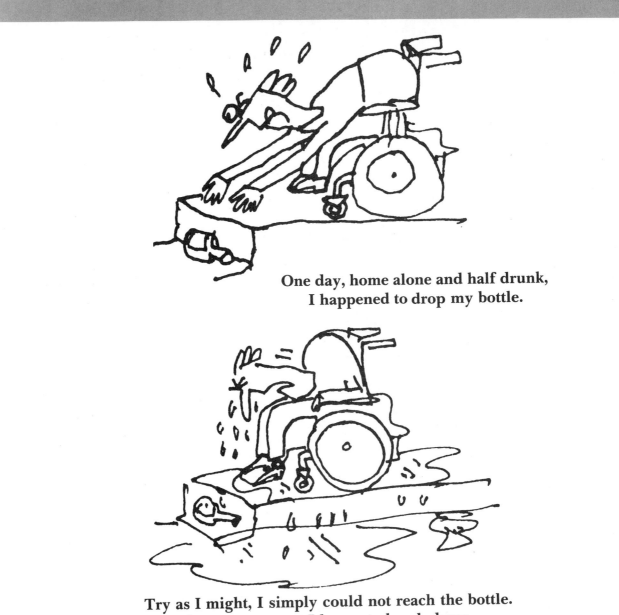

One day, home alone and half drunk,
I happened to drop my bottle.

Try as I might, I simply could not reach the bottle.
I became so upset I began to break down.

I began screaming and didn't care who heard me. I
was so frustrated I began screaming at God, who I didn't
even believe in.

As I raved I felt the anguish of my entire life. I cried
a deep and cleansing cry, like a child. At the same time I felt
strangely comforted. From that time till now I have not wanted
a drink. I rolled to the telephone and called for help.

In treatment I learned that it was alcoholism that made me drink, not my difficult life experiences...

I'm not sure what caused my alcoholism, but I think
heredity played a role in it.

Though I am sober, my basic personality has not changed.

And I found a new way of living which really works...

even in tough times.